D0757601

EXPLORERS!

Francisco Pizarro

Explorer of South America

Sandra J. Kachurek

Enslow Publishers, Inc.

40 Industrial Road   PO Box 38
Box 398   Aldershot
Berkeley Heights, NJ 07922   Hants GU12 6BP
USA   UK

http://www.enslow.com

Library of Congress Cataloging-in-Publication Data

Kachurek, Sandra J.
    Francisco Pizarro : explorer of South America / Sandra J. Kachurek.
        p. cm. — (Explorers!)
    Summary: An introduction to the life of Spanish explorer and soldier, Francisco Pizarro, and his conquest of the Inca Empire in Peru.
    Includes bibliographical references and index.
    ISBN 0-7660-2178-5
    1. Pizarro, Francisco, ca. 1475–1541—Juvenile literature. 2. Peru—History—Conquest, 1522–1548—Juvenile literature. 3. South America—Discovery and exploration—Spanish—Juvenile literature. 4. Governors—Peru—Biography—Juvenile literature. 5. Explorers—Peru—Biography—Juvenile literature. 6. Explorers—South America—Biography—Juvenile literature. 7. Explorers—Spain—Biography—Juvenile literature. [1. Pizarro, Francisco, ca. 1475–1541. 2. Explorers. 3. Peru—History—Conquest, 1522–1548. 4. Incas. 5. Indians of South America—Peru.] I. Title. II. Explorers! (Enslow Publishers)
    F3442.P776K33   2004
    985'.02'092—dc22

                                    2003014172

Printed in the United States of America

10 9 8 7 6 5 4 3 2 1

To Our Readers: We have done our best to make sure all Internet Addresses in this book were active and appropriate when we went to press. However, the author and the publisher have no control over and assume no liability for the material available on those Internet sites or on other Web sites they may link to. Any comments or suggestions can be sent by e-mail to comments@enslow.com or to the address on the back cover.

Every effort has been made to locate all copyright holders of material used in this book. If any errors or omissions have occurred, corrections will be made in future editions of this book.

Illustration Credits: © 1996–2004 ArtToday, Inc., pp. 1, 8, 9, 22 (four insets), 24 (background and bottom), 26, 27, 30 (three insets), 32, 43 (top and bottom); © 1999 Artville, LLC., pp. 10, 16, 33; Corel Corporation, pp. 6, 18, 21, 22 (background), 28, 30 (background), 36 (bottom), 41; Enslow Publishers, Inc., p. 40; Enslow Publishers, Inc., using © 1999 Artville, LLC. map, p. 4; Library of Congress, pp. 4 (portrait), 7, 12, 14, 20, 23, 24 (portrait), 31, 34, 36 (top), 39, 42.

Cover Illustration: background, Monster Zero Media; portrait, Library of Congress.

Please note: Compasses on the cover and in the book are from © 1999 Artville, LLC.

Contents

1 A Battle for Gold 5

2 Two Early Voyages 11

3 March to Peru 19

4 A Roomful of Gold 25

5 Governor of Peru 29

6 Pizarro's Death 37

Timeline 44

Words to Know 45

Learn More About Francisco Pizarro
(Books and Internet Addresses) 46

Index 48

List of Maps

Map	Page
Pizzaro's Routes	4
Spain	10
South America	16
Peru	33
Spanish Explorations and Conquests	40

CARIBBEAN SEA

Panama

Panama City

Venezuela

Colombia

1531   1524

1526

Isla del Gallo

Ecuador

1527

Tumbes

Cajamarca

1528

Peru

Lima
FOUNDED
IN 1535

1533

Cuzco

PACIFIC OCEAN

Francisco Pizarro led the conquest of the Inca Empire in the 1500s.

A Battle for Gold

Francisco Pizarro marched to the center of the city with over a hundred Spanish soldiers. Some soldiers rode horses, and some soldiers walked on foot.

It took two months of marching for the men to reach the city. Pizarro thought he would be attacked by the Inca armies and their leader, Atahualpa (ah-tah-WAHL-pah). But, the Spaniards were left alone.

Pizarro did not like where they were. The place was empty and quiet. The center of the city had walls on all sides, and the only way out was two gates.

Francisco Pizarro knew where Atahualpa's soldiers

were, and he knew how many there were. In the hills around the city, between five thousand and six thousand Inca men were ready to battle. They were the best fighters who used clubs, slings, and axes as weapons.

Pizarro sent some men to meet Atahualpa. The men came back with a message from Atahualpa. He said he would meet them the next day. He said his men would have no weapons.

The first to get there were two thousand Inca men who served the

Ruins from the Inca Empire remain today in Peru.

king. Next came a hundred dancers and singers. They came before the Inca princes. Then slaves came into the city and swept the roads for the men who carried the Inca king Atahualpa.

Francisco Pizarro had a plan. A Spanish priest greeted the king and spoke about the Christian God. The priest gave the king a Bible.

King Atahualpa had never seen a book before. He did not know what to do with it. He threw it down. When he did this, Pizarro and his men attacked.

The Inca did not plan well. Many Inca men were jammed into the small center of the city. They could not

Atahualpa was the leader of the Inca.

Pizarro sent men to meet Atahualpa.

move. They were killed very easily. The Spaniards had guns, swords, and horses.

Francisco Pizarro fought his way to the Inca king. A Spanish soldier was ready to kill Atahualpa with his sword. Pizarro stopped him. He grabbed the king's arm and led him away. The battle was over.

Pizarro did not hurt Atahualpa. He took him to one of the palaces in the city. King Atahualpa promised to fill a palace room with gold. Then Pizarro said he would set Atahualpa free.

At once, more gold than any Spaniard had ever seen began to fill the room.

Francisco Pizarro's dream had come true. For more than eight years, he had explored this land in search of gold and treasure. Now he could hold it in his hands.

The Inca and the Spaniards fought. Because Pizarro wanted gold and treasure, he captured Atahualpa and, at first, did not harm him.

Francisco Pizarro was born in Spain around 1474.

Two Early Voyages

Francisco Pizarro was born around 1474 in Trujillo, Spain. No one knows exactly when he was born. The date was not written down. His father was a captain of infantry. His parents never married each other. His mother, Francisca Gonzalez, was happy when her son got a job. Little Francisco fed the neighbor's pigs for money. Francisco never went to school so he did not learn to read and write.

When he was a young man, Pizarro was a soldier in Spain's army. He became a good leader. Soldiers wanted to work for him, but he wanted to explore. In 1502,

Vasco Núñez de Balboa was the first European to see the Pacific Ocean.

Pizarro sailed for the island of Hispaniola in the Caribbean Sea. He lived there for a few years.

In 1509, Pizarro sailed with Alonso de Ojeda from Spain. They explored the coast of Venezuela in South America. Pizarro also went with Vasco Núñez de Balboa to explore the country of Panama in Central America. In 1513, Pizarro became one of the first Europeans to see the Pacific Ocean.

On the trip with Balboa, Pizarro heard about the Inca. He heard that the Inca had lots of gold and treasure.

In 1524, Pizarro led a trip of discovery. He had eighty men and two ships. He had food, weapons, and horses. He hoped to find Peru and its gold and treasure.

Pizarro and his men landed in Colombia. They went south. They searched for three years, looking for the Inca Empire. They did not find anything.

Many men died. Some men died from sickness and hunger. Some men died in small battles with Indians. One time, Pizarro was hurt badly and almost died.

Pizarro went back to Panama. He wanted more men

and supplies. Not many men wanted to sail with him. Pizarro could not get any money for supplies, but he did not give up.

He sailed again for Peru in 1526. He stopped on the coast of Ecuador. The search for gold and treasure was hard. The men wanted to go back. Pizarro took twelve men, some supplies, and horses. They stayed on an island called Isla del Gallo. They stayed there for five months. Pizarro would not go back to the ship. One ship left for Panama without Pizarro. He and his twelve men were alone.

Pizarro spoke to his men. He said he

Pizarro wanted to find gold and treasure. He landed on the coast of Ecuador.

hurt, too. He told them he knew they would find the Inca and the treasure.

One day, one of the men saw a big trading raft made from balsa wood. It was from the city of Tumbes. There were six people in the boat from Peru called Peruvians. They had gold and cloth.

Pizarro was happy. He and his men went to Tumbes. They found gold and treasure in Tumbes. They took it to their ship and sailed back to Panama.

The people in Tumbes were scared. They never saw men like Pizarro before. The Tumbes people sent runners to the Inca king. His name was Huayna Capac. The runners told King Capac about Pizarro. They told how he looked. The Spaniards looked wild to the Inca. They had never seen men with white faces and beards. The Inca called the Spaniards, "Bearded Ones."

They also told Capac about the horses that Pizarro and his men rode. They had never seen horses. They thought they were monsters.

Guyana

Venezuela

Suriname

Colombia

French Guiana

Brazil

Ecuador

Bolivia

Peru

Paraguay

Chile

Argentina

Uruguay

The Spaniards explored the countries of Venezuela, Peru, and Colombia in South America.

SOUTH AMERICA

King Capac was worried. He was sad. Soon after hearing the news, he got sick with smallpox and died. His son, Atahualpa, became king of the Inca Empire.

Pizarro made it home to Panama. The people in Panama were very glad to see the treasure from Tumbes. Now they wanted Pizarro to go back to Peru to find the Inca. They hoped to get more gold and treasure.

The Inca Empire was located in the Andes Mountains of South America.

March to Peru

The king of Spain honored Francisco Pizarro for his work as an explorer. The king enjoyed Pizarro's stories about his search for gold. He named Pizarro commander in chief of all his trips. The king told Pizarro he could rule over any land he conquered in Peru.

Pizarro wanted to go back to Peru and look for the Inca and their treasure. He needed ships, men, and supplies for his third trip. He had help from some friends, Diego de Almagro and Hernando de Luque.

Pizarro's brothers came. His cousin, Pedro Pizarro,

Pizarro talked to the king of Spain. The king was pleased with Pizarro's stories of gold and treasure.

came, too. He was fifteen years old. He took notes of everything he saw.

Pizarro also had an interpreter. The interpreter was a young boy from Peru. His name was Don Martin. The boy learned to speak Spanish quickly. Now he could tell Pizarro what the people in Peru said.

In January 1531, Pizarro left Panama for Peru. Pizarro was sixty years old. He had two ships, over a hundred men, and thirty-seven horses. They explored along the coast of Peru.

They made small trips into Peru. One stop was on an island called Puná. They fought with the Puná Indians. The Puná lost and ran away. The Spaniards stayed in Puná for a few months, but it was time to find the Inca Empire.

On September 14, 1532, Pizarro took some of his men and horses and began the long march in search of the Inca treasures.

The travel was hard. Pizarro and his men crossed marshy jungles and swam wide rivers. They walked over mountains and through deserts. When some men got sick, other men pulled them on rafts.

Pizarro kept waiting for an attack by the Inca soldiers.

Pizarro and his men had to travel through jungles and rivers.

The Inca built roads leading in and out of their towns.

When they walked into villages, Pizarro asked if anyone knew what the king was doing. No one would tell him.

Pizarro's march got easier. The Inca had built paved roads. The roads were easy to walk on. They had high walls on both sides and were shaded by trees. There were places to rest along the way.

Pizarro's men were worried. They feared they would be attacked at any time. Pizarro gave them the courage to go on.

But Pizarro's men were worried. They feared an attack at any time. Pizarro was a good leader who controlled his army well. He gave them hope to go on.

On November 15, 1532, Pizarro stopped and looked down. He saw the valley of Cajamarca—the city where the Inca king waited.

Soon Pizarro would have to fight the Inca.

Pizarro finally found the Inca
Empire. He led his men to battle
and conquered the Inca.

A Roomful of Gold

The battle with the Inca came when Pizarro and his men reached the center of the city of Cajamarca. It was very crowded. Pizarro's army killed thousands of unarmed Inca men. When Pizarro captured King Atahualpa, the battle was over.

King Atahualpa agreed to fill a room full of gold and treasure for his freedom. He would also fill two rooms full of silver. He said he could fill the rooms in two months.

Soon, all the gold and silver objects that the Inca people had in their city were carried to the king's room.

There were many jewels and gold plates. The Inca brought vases, jars, and pots of gold. Chairs and water fountains that weighed over two hundred pounds in gold were added to the treasure pile.

Some of Pizarro's men wrote down every object. Sometimes the treasure came so quickly that they could not write it down fast enough.

This Inca tapestry shows King Atahualpa and his attendants.

Pizarro's two ships could not hold all the treasure. Pizarro had the Inca melt the gold and silver into shapes that were easy to carry and store, called ingots. Each day, the Inca melted down over 440 pounds of gold into ingots.

Later the gold was given to the Spanish men and leaders. The king of Spain was given one fifth of the gold. Pizarro kept the most gold. He had over $3 million.

Months passed. Pizarro wanted more gold. He told King Atahualpa to get more gold fast. The king told Pizarro of other cities in Peru that had gold. Pizarro ordered his men to find these cities.

Before he left to look for more gold, Pizarro had King Atahualpa killed.

Pizarro kept Atahualpa alive for many months, but Pizarro wanted more gold. Before he left to look for more, he had Atahualpa killed.

Pizarro sent his men to find more gold. They found beautiful Inca cities. This is what is left of an ancient Inca town in Peru.

Governor of Peru

After killing King Atahualpa, Francisco Pizarro sent his men to Cuzco. Cuzco was the capital city of the Inca Empire. All the Inca kings had lived in Cuzco.

When the Spaniards got to Cuzco, they had to stop and stare. The city was beautiful. The buildings and gardens honored the Inca kings. The city shined with gold. The Spaniards had never seen anything like it.

Pizarro's men wanted to take over Cuzco. They wanted the gold. The men fought the Incas. Again the Spanish army was very strong. They won the battle and

Inca cities seemed to shine with gold and treasure. The Spaniards had never seen anything like it.

took over the city. They took away all the gold that they could find.

Francisco Pizarro lived in the best house in Cuzco. He lived in the palace where the Inca kings once lived.

Cuzco was Pizarro's place of command. He sent soldiers to fight the Inca in other cities. The Spaniards won every battle. Soon, the Spaniards ruled most of the Inca Empire.

Some of the men went back to Spain. The men told Spanish king Charles I

Pizarro made a grand entrance into the city of Cuzco.

about Pizarro's discoveries. The men gave King Charles gold. The king was happy. He sent more soldiers and supplies to Peru.

The king also told the men that Francisco Pizarro was now the governor of Peru. The king said that Pizarro's friend Diego de Almagro was the governor of Chile.

When Almagro got the news, he was angry. He said he wanted to rule in Peru. But he took some men and went to Chile. He hoped to find gold in Chile.

After a battle with the Inca, Pizarro and the Spaniards ruled the city.

Pizarro was now governor of Peru. He wanted a capital city near the sea. When Spanish ships came with people and supplies, they could get to the capital city more easily if it were by the seacoast.

In January 1535, Pizarro found flat land near the shores of Peru. In Spanish, he called the land El Ciudad de Los Reyes or the "City of the Kings." He named the city after the three kings who had visited the baby Jesus.

The land was by a river that the Inca called Rimac. The Spanish called it Lima. Everyone began to call the capital city Lima, too.

Pizarro planned the city. The streets were wide. A Catholic cathedral, a government building, and the richest houses stood in the center of the city.

After Pizarro set up his home in Peru, many people sailed from Spain to settle in Peru.

Pizarro's house was built in the center of the city. He put in large gardens behind his house. He grew fruits, vegetables, and flowers. Thousands of Inca people worked in the gardens.

As Pizarro began to build Lima, he founded another city. The new city was not too far away from Lima. Pizarro named the new city Trujillo, after the town in Spain where he was born.

Peru was fast becoming a Spanish country.

The Inca method of terrace farming can be seen today in areas of Peru. In mountainous areas, people carved steps into the mountain so it was easier to farm.

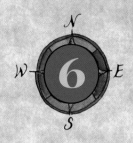

Pizarro's Death

Many people in Spain and other Spanish countries heard about the treasures in Peru. They heard how much gold Pizarro had found. They, too, wanted to be rich. They left their homes and sailed to Peru. Some of the Spaniards thought they would quickly find gold and go back home. But many of them chose to stay in Peru.

The new Spanish settlers sent for their family and friends to come to Peru. They moved into the new cities of Lima and Trujillo. They also moved into the old Inca cities like Cuzco.

The settlers brought animals and plants from home.

They brought donkeys, pigs, cattle, and sheep. They planted wheat, grapes, and turnips. They started gold and silver mines. The mines went into the mountains and underneath the ground. Inca slaves climbed into deep tunnels to take out the gold and silver from under the ground.

Not everyone was happy.

In 1537, Pizarro's friend Diego de Almagro came back from Chile. He did not find gold, and he did not want to rule Chile. He wanted to rule parts of Peru.

Almagro was angry with Pizarro. Almagro and his men wanted to fight Pizarro for some of Pizarro's power. Pizarro did not want to fight his friend. Pizarro said that Almagro could rule the city of Cuzco.

There was peace for a while. Then Almagro became angry again because he wanted more power. He and his soldiers started a battle with Pizarro and his men. Almagro lost, and he was captured and killed. Almagro's friends would not forget what Pizarro had done. They planned to kill Pizarro one day.

Pizarro and Diego de Almagro were once friends but Almagro was unhappy. Almagro wanted more power and soon started a battle. Pizarro won and captured and killed Almagro.

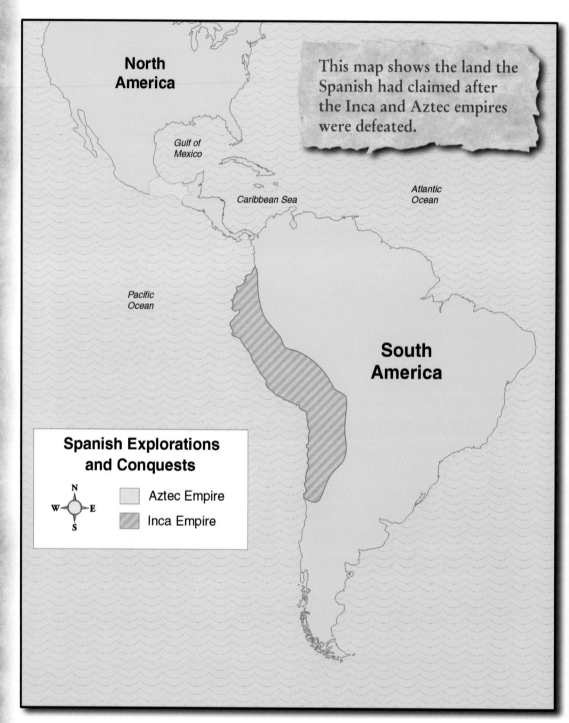

This map shows the land the Spanish had claimed after the Inca and Aztec empires were defeated.

North America

Gulf of Mexico

Caribbean Sea

Atlantic Ocean

Pacific Ocean

South America

Spanish Explorations and Conquests

N
W · E
S

Aztec Empire

Inca Empire

Francisco Pizarro now ruled over all of Peru. He lived like a prince in a big house in Lima. His brothers were in charge of other cities in Peru.

Pizarro's men still fought the Inca. The Inca who were not killed or did not run away were made into slaves. Some Spanish people had over four thousand Inca slaves working on their farms.

The Spanish people treated the Inca slaves cruelly. The Spaniards made the Inca work hard

Inca ruins in Peru show how skilled the Inca were in building homes and roads.

every day, all day long, with no rest. The Inca were not fed well. They were punished in cruel ways. Many Inca died from disease and from working too hard.

In 1541, Francisco Pizarro was killed. Diego de Almagro's son and other men were angry at Pizarro for killing Almagro. One Sunday afternoon, the men rushed into Pizarro's house and stabbed him.

After his death, the king of Spain sent other men to replace Pizarro as ruler of Peru.

Because of Pizarro, Peru had become a strong Spanish country. The work of Spanish explorers like Francisco Pizarro was famous.

Almagro's son and friends made plans to kill Pizarro. In 1541, Pizarro was killed.

People believed that the Spanish explorers and soldiers were the best in the world.

Pizarro opened up South America for Spanish settlers. In doing that, the Inca and their way of life were destroyed. What remains today are ancient ruins and pottery that historians have found.

Pizarro helped tell the story of early Peru when the Inca ruled. Pizarro brought men with him who wrote down everything they saw. Their notes tell about the Inca people and how they lived. Later, their notes were made into books. People still read those books today.

Francisco Pizarro will be remembered as an explorer and conqueror of South American lands.

Timeline

Around 1474—Francisco Pizarro is born in Trujillo, Spain.

1513—Sails the Caribbean Sea with Vasco Núñez de Balboa.

November 14, 1524—Leads his first sailing voyage toward Peru.

1527—Inca king Huayna Capac dies.

1528-29—The king of Spain honors Pizarro as commander in chief in Peru.

1530—The Inca crown Atahualpa king.

November 15, 1532—Pizarro enters Cajamarca, captures Atahualpa.

August 29, 1533—Atahualpa is killed.

January 1535—Pizarro begins to build Lima, Peru.

1538—Diego de Almagro is killed by Pizarro's men.

June 1541—Francisco Pizarro is murdered by friends of Almagro.

Words to Know

balsa—A raft made from reeds; also a strong lightweight wood.

command—A group of troops.

conquer—To take over land or people by fighting.

explorer—One who travels little known seas or lands.

governor—One who rules.

infantry—A section of an army, whose soldiers are trained to fight on foot.

ingot—A block of metal, like silver or gold, that is cast into a shape that is easy to store.

interpreter—One who explains the meaning of words of a different language.

settlers—People who make their home in a new country.

slave—A person who is owned by another person.

Learn More About
Francisco Pizarro

Books

Bergen, Lara Rice. *Francisco Pizarro*. Austin, Tex.: Raintree Steck-Vaughn Publishers, 2000.

DeAngelis, Gina. *Francisco Pizarro and the Conquest of the Inca*. New York: Chelsea House Publishers, 2000.

Donaldson-Forbes, Jeff. *Francisco Pizarro*. Rosen Publishing Group, Inc., 2001.

Jacobs, William Jay. *Pizarro, Conqueror of Peru*. New York: Franklin Watts, 1994.

Marrin, Albert. *Inca and Spaniard: Pizarro and the Conquests of Peru*. New York: Atheneum, 1989.

Nishi, Dennis. *The Inca Empire*. San Diego, Calif.: Lucent Books, 2000.

Learn More About
Francisco Pizarro

Internet Addresses

Conquistadors

<http://www.pbs.org/conquistadors/pizarro/pizarro_
flat.html>

*Find out more about Pizarro and the Spanish
conquistadors at this site.*

Francisco Pizarro: Explorer

<http://www.enchantedlearning.com/explorers/page/
p/pizarro.shtml>

Learn more about Pizarro from Enchanted Learning.

Index

A
Andes Mountains, 18
Atahualpa, 5–9, 17, 25, 27, 29
Aztec Empire, 40

B
balsa wood, 15
Bible, 7

C
Cajamarca, 23, 25
Capac, Huayna, 15, 17
Caribbean Sea, 13
Central America, 13
Charles I, 31–32
Chile, 32, 38
Colombia, 13, 16
Cuzco, 29, 31, 37, 38

D
de Almagro, Diego, 19, 32, 38, 39, 42
de Luque, Hernando, 19
de Ojeda, Alonso, 13

E
Ecuador, 14
El Ciudad de Los Reyes, 33

G
Gonzalez, Francisca, 11

H
Hispaniola, 13

I
Inca Empire, 4, 17, 20, 29, 31, 40
ingots, 26
Isla del Gallo, 14

L
Lima, Peru, 33, 35, 37, 41

M
Martin, Don, 20

N
Núñez de Balboa, Vasco, 13

P
Panama, 13, 14, 15, 16, 17, 20
Peru, 13, 14, 19, 20, 32, 33, 37, 38, 41, 42
Pizarro, Pedro, 19
Puná Indians, 20

R
Rimac, 33

S
Spain, 10, 11, 13, 31

T
Trujillo, Peru, 35, 37
Trujillo, Spain, 11
Tumbes, Peru, 15, 17

V
Venezuela, 16